LEARN ENGLISH THROUGH SONG

Text/Workbook
Level One

Millie Grenough

Technical Review:
Manuel C.R. Dos Santos
ELT Consultant/Author

McGRAW-HILL

Mexico, Santafe de Bogota, Buenos Aires, Caracas, Guatemala, Lisbon
Madrid, New York, Panama, San Juan, Sao Paulo,
Auckland, Hamburg, London, Milan, Montreal, New Delhi,
Paris, San Francisco, St. Louis, Sydney, Singapore, Tokyo, Toronto

Developmental Editor: Louise Jennewine

Publishing Coordinator: Janet Gomolson

Permissions Coordinator: Lowell Britson

Design: Jorge Martínez

Music Engraving: Tony Finno, Joe Muccioli and the King Brand Company

SING IT! LEARN ENGLISH THROUGH SONG. Level One

Copyright © 1993 by Millie Grenough. All rights reserved. Published and distributed throughout the world by McGraw-Hill, Inc. Printed in Mexico. Except as permitted under the United States Copyright Act of 1976, no part of this publication may be reproduced or distributed in any form or by any means or stored in a data base or retrieval system, without the prior written permission of the publisher.

ISBN: 07-024705-6 Text/Workbook, Level One
07-024706-4 Cassette, Level One

3456789012   P.E.–93   9087643215

Impreso en México   Printed in Mexico

Esta obra se terminó de
imprimir en Junio de 1995 en
Litográfica Eros, S.A. de C.V.
Calz. Tlatilco Núm. 78
Col. Tlatilco
Delegación Azcapotzalco
02860 México, D.F.

Se tiraron 3,500 ejemplares

SING IT!
LEARN ENGLISH
THROUGH SONG

*is dedicated to the spirit of song
in all of us.*

ABOUT THE AUTHOR

MILLIE GRENOUGH grew up in a singing family in Kentucky, learned Spanish from people and songs in Bolivia, Colombia, Mexico, Nicaragua, Panama, Peru, Puerto Rico and Spain, and has taught English as a Foreign and Second Language to people from more than twenty countries. Millie is also a Clinical Social Worker and a professional singer. She is co-producer of the cassette "MOSAIC: New Haven Sings of Peace and War" and has developed teaching curricula for Headstart, Adult Basic Education Programs, the Instituto de Estudios Norteamericanos in Barcelona and the International Relations Center at Yale University.

CONTENTS

Preface IX
Special Notes for Everyone XI
Special Notes for Teachers XIII
Special Notes for Students XV
Special Notes for Students without Teachers XIX
Acknowledgments and Thanks XXI
Acknowledgments for Songs XXIII

1. COLOURS 1

Key Structures
- **Present Tense:** verb to be and others
- **Adverb:** rarely
- **Expressions:** mm-hmm, uh-huh
- **Possessive Adjectives**
- **Reductions**

Communicative Objectives
- To describe people
- To talk about colors and various objects
- To express feeling

2. DEEP IN THE HEART OF TEXAS 5

Key Structures
- **Present Tense:** verb to be and others
- **Adjectives:** big and others
- **Definite Article:** the
- **"Is like"**
- **Prepositions:** in, along and others

Communicative Objectives
- To describe your birthplace or hometown
- To talk about cowboys
- To describe things using definite article and adjectives

3. MICHAEL, ROW THE BOAT ASHORE 9

Key Structures
- **Imperative:** affirmative and negative
- **Phrasal Verb:** wipe away
- **Definite Article:** the and others
- **Indefinite Article:** a
- **Gerund as Adjective:** helping hand
- **Times of Day:** night, morn

Communicative Objectives
- To talk about family members
- To give orders and commands
- To describe what you do in the morning and at night

4. TAKE ME OUT TO THE BALL GAME 13

Key Structures
- **Imperative:** take me out and others
- **Present Tense:** contracted form (it's); negative (don't)

	Phrasal Vebs: take me out; never get back	
	Adverb: never	
	Numbers: one, two, three	
Communicative Objectives	To discuss baseball and your favorite players	
	To state your preferences in food and drink	
	To explain your likes and dislikes	

5. ROCK MY SOUL 17

Key Structures	**Imperative:** rock my soul
	Present Tense: I'm in the bosom and others
	Modal: I can feel the light
	Adjectives: high, low, dark and others
	Gerunds as Adjectives: towering man, light shining
	"Oh" as Exclamation: Oh, rock my soul!
	Prepositions: over, under and others
	So + Adjective: so high, so wide and others
Communicative Objectives	To talk about heroes and heroines
	To identify places
	To create rhymes

6. THERE'S A HOLE 22

Key Structures	**Present Tense:** there's a hole and others
	Prepositions: on, in, of
	There is/there's
Communicative Objectives	To talk about many objects at the same time
	To tell what is here and to state its exact location

7. TURN! TURN! TURN! 26

Key Structures	**Imperative:** Turn!
	Phrasal Verbs: build up, break down and others
	There is
	"to" + Adjective: it's not too late
Communicative Objectives	To find synonyms (words that mean the same thing) and opposites
	To describe excess using "too"
	To talk about seasons and months of the year

8. SHALOM CHAVERIM (We Wish You Peace) 30

Key Structures	**Present Tense:** we wish you peace and others
	Relatives: all of your kin
	Till = until: till we meet again
Communicative Objectives	To explore ways to say words in different languages
	To identify relatives (aunts, uncles, cousins) and talk about them
	To discuss songs from your own country

9. HE'S GOT THE WHOLE WORLD 34

- **Key Structures**
  - **"Got" = has:** He's got the whole world
  - **Adjectives:** the whole world, the little-bitty baby
- **Communicative Objectives**
  - To talk about traditional African-American songs
  - To identify what you and others have

10. AS TEARS GO BY 38

- **Key Structures**
  - **Present Tense:** I sit and watch and others
  - **Modals:** affirmative (I can see); negative (my riches can't buy)
  - **"Used to" + Verb:** things I used to do
- **Communicative Objectives**
  - To talk about what people are doing now
  - To discuss things you usually do and when you do them (times of day)
  - To describe things you used to do (in the past)

11. WHEN THE SAINTS GO MARCHING IN 42

- **Key Structures**
  - **Present Tense:** sun refuses to shine
  - **Phrasal Verbs:** goes down; go marching in
  - **Verb + to + Verb:** I want to be in that number
- **Communicative Objectives**
  - To identify who is doing what
  - To talk about refusing to do something

12. DRY BONES 46

- **Key Structures**
  - **Future with "going to":** those bones are going to rise again
  - **Imperative:** hear the word of the Lord!
  - **Parts of Body:** toe bone, heel bone and others
- **Communicative Objectives**
  - To identify various parts of the body
  - To talk about what you are going to do
  - To create activities to practice new knowledge

13. RHYTHM IS GONNA GET YOU 50

- **Key Structures**
  - **Future with "going to":** rhythm is gonna get you
  - **Imperative:** Throw the covers on your head
  - **Phrasal Verb:** turn off all the lights
  - **Non-standard English:** pretend like you are dead; it don't matter
- **Communicative Objectives**
  - To discuss music and your relationship to it
  - To identify things that you can "turn off" and "turn on"
  - To create a publicity story about what you are going to do

Artist Index 55
Genre and Theme Index 56
Grammatical Index 59
Song Index 64

PREFACE

Why sing English?
Because music gets into our subconscious quickly and subtly, and because songs are a powerful medium for acquiring new knowledge and for reinforcing already-learned structures.

Throughout the world, English is probably encountered more often today in music than on the printed page. English students in Mexico City, Rio de Janeiro or Tokyo may hear little spoken English outside their English classes, but all of them are exposed to American and English songs on radio, TV, and in movies. Many of them are familiar with traditional folk and spiritual melodies and even sing these songs in their native languages. These people, as well as new arrivals in New York or London, readily tune in to songs. Once they are introduced to specific songs, they practice, consciously or unconsciously, for many hours outside class.

SING IT!, First Edition helped many people learn English. Since the response to the first edition was so positive, many of the songs and the structure that made SING IT! successful and fun to use have been retained. Suggestions from teachers and students encouraged me to add the following features in this expanded six-level series:

- **New songs,** including pop favorites from the 1960s, 1970s, 1980s and 1990s
- **International flavor** and **multi-cultural focus,** including songs and artists from around the world
- Extensive **Learning Ideas** and **Exercises** for each song
- **Photos and bios of composers and artists,** from Gloria Estefan and Billie Holiday to Michael Jackson and John Lennon
- **Newly-recorded cassettes,** with full music and spoken introductions for each song, for classroom and home use.

Out of many possible songs, eighty specific ones were selected for the following reasons:

- **Enjoyment.** The melodies are often familiar and can be sung easily by individuals or groups. The accompanying cassettes provide a professional back-up that invites people to sing along easily. The music is up-beat and fun to follow.
- **Clarity.** The words of the songs introduce and reinforce vocabulary and grammatical patterns in a meaningful and easy-to-remember context. The lyrics appear both in the text/workbook and on the cassettes. Words on the cassettes are crisp and clear, yet follow natural pronunciation.

- **Learning value.** The songs have been carefully chosen to illustrate particular verb tenses, grammatical structures and vocabulary. Each song has a listing of the Key Structures as well as Teaching and Learning Ideas and exercises.

The eighty songs are sequenced according to grammar and vocabulary, progressing from elementary to more advanced English. Each level, consisting of a Text/Workbook and Cassette, contains songs focusing on specific verb tenses and grammatical usages:

- **Level One:** Present Tense (verb **to be** & others), Imperative, Future with "going to"
- **Level Two:** Present Continuous, Future with "'ll," "will" and "shall"
- **Level Three:** Simple Past; Comparisons ("like," "as," comparative and superlative adjectives)
- **Level Four:** Other Past Tenses (Past Continuous, Present Perfect, Past Perfect)
- **Level Five:** Conditionals, If, Modals, Wish
- **Level Six:** Grand review of all verb tenses; Clauses; Non-standard English; Complete Index.

See the **Special Notes** sections which follow for more specific information on using **SING IT! LEARN ENGLISH THROUGH SONG** as a student or teacher. Have fun, whether you are in class or learning English on your own!

SPECIAL NOTES FOR EVERYONE

SING IT! LEARN ENGLISH THROUGH SONG is for you:

- to enjoy
- to improve your listening skills
- to increase your vocabulary
- to sharpen your pronunciation
- to improve your speaking ability
- to enliven your knowledge and use of grammatical structures
- to heighten your memory
- to make you more comfortable with use of expressions, phrases and slang
- to challenge your creativity

Twenty-five years ago I discovered that songs helped me learn a new language. Now scientists say that what I found out by personal experience is true. They say that songs enter our brains in a different way than spoken or printed things, that they go to a different part of the brain, and that they often sink in there deeply. That is why you may suddenly remember a phrase from a song that you haven't heard since you were much younger. Furthermore, scientific tests reveal that when both hemispheres of the brain are working at the same time, as they are when you participate in learning a song, the learning is more complete and longer-lasting.

In **SING IT! LEARN ENGLISH THROUGH SONG,** I invite you to learn English more easily and more enjoyably in a manner that will stay with you for years. I hope you have fun as you learn!

SPECIAL NOTES FOR TEACHERS

You can use SING IT! LEARN ENGLISH THROUGH SONG in many ways:

- to begin, extend or end a class
- to illustrate a particular structure you are introducing
- to reinforce and review material that you have already taught
- as a take-off point for class discussion or for oral presentations by individual students or groups of students. For example: "What song in your country does this remind you of?" "Can you tell more about a particular song that you like?", etc.
- as a lead-in for compositions, essay questions or creative writing.

You can use the cassettes to introduce and to practice the songs in the classroom. In **Special Notes for Students** and **Special Notes for Students without Teachers** which follow this section, ideas on how to use the cassettes for active listening are given.

You can also encourage students to listen to the spoken **Introductions** and songs on their own, and then practice by repeating the Introductions and singing the songs along with the cassette. Students may practice with each other or alone, in class and at home.

A complete listing of the **Key Structures** used in each song is included so that you may select a song according to what you wish to teach on a particular day. In Key Structures we include verb usages, other grammar, expressions and sometimes also key vocabulary. Look for Key Structures as they appear in song lyrics; they are highlighted in color. Verb usages are always listed first in Key Structures sections. Other grammatical structures appear in alphabetical order after verb usages. You may want to teach the structure before the class hears the song, or after. Either way works.

The listing of **Communicative Objectives** tells you, at a glance, topics and structures that you can develop and practice in conversation and in writing.

The **Learning Ideas** provide an opportunity for you to help expand students' vocabulary, to see if they understand the content of the song and to learn new grammatical structures. Extensive Learning Ideas for each song are included. You do not need to do all of them; feel free to adapt them or invent your own. Invite the students to make up their own questions and answers. If you wish, you may use the Learning Ideas as homework assignments, or for a group of students to complete as you are working with another part of the class. Note that the Extra Learning sections may be too difficult for some students. We include them as an extra challenge for eager students.

An **Answer Key** is available as a supplement to this book.

Footnotes help explain certain difficult words or structures. For example, the word *gonna* is numbered[1] and explained with a footnote as the reduction of *going to*. Also when a more difficult verb tense appears in a simpler song, it is briefly explained in a footnote.

Obviously, songs are written by poets and are not designed to teach English—but learning English through song adds variety and challenge for teacher and student. Even though a song appears in Level One, it may contain a few words or structures that are more difficult. Likewise, a song in Level Six may contain some simpler tenses and vocabulary. This need not be a problem! When exposed to difficult structures and vocabulary, students often have fun trying to infer meaning from the context. Likewise, more advanced students enjoy recognizing basic structures embedded in more challenging structures.

The four **Indexes** are designed to help you and your students. Use them yourself to find songs to illustrate particular points of grammar or to choose a theme for class discussion. Show your students how to use the indexes (fuller suggestions are given in the **Special Notes for Students** section). Have them practice looking up an artist or a song. This provides good experience in alphabetizing, using telephone books, and in doing research.

If you have a mixed-level class, or decide to bring several classes together for an occasion, songs are a good way to involve students of various levels at the same time. The elementary students can listen, sing along and pick up new knowledge. The more advanced students have the chance to "teach" and demonstrate their understanding to the rest of the class.

You may choose a song from any section simply because it appeals to you or your class, or because you are practicing a particular structure. Feel free to move around between the levels and use songs as you wish.

SPECIAL NOTES FOR STUDENTS

When I was trying to learn a new language–Spanish–I had a very difficult time. I paid attention in class and did my homework, but I still had a hard time pronouncing words correctly and remembering verb structures and grammar. To relax and give my brain a break, I began listening to songs from Spanish-speaking countries on the radio and on cassettes. Before I knew it, I was beginning to understand certain phrases and was able to sing along with little portions of the songs.

I decided to ask my teacher to help me out. I said to her, "If I record some songs in Spanish, will you help me figure out the parts that I don't understand?" She agreed to the idea. So, day after day, I listened to my favorite songs, and, day after day, I began learning more Spanish.

At first, I chose easier songs because I couldn't understand songs with too many words or verbs that were very difficult. Gradually my Spanish grew. Then one week in class we were trying to learn the subjunctive and I just couldn't get it. That night I happened to listen to the song "Bésame Mucho" and I heard the words "como si fuera esta noche la última vez..." Suddenly I really heard "...como si fuera..." and I realized, "Ah, so that's the subjunctive!" I have never forgotten it.

So that is why, when I began teaching English, I decided to use songs as part of my teaching. My students came from many different countries: Brazil, Czechoslovakia, China, Colombia, France, Greece, Italy, Israel, Japan, Kenya, Mexico, Panama, Peru, Poland, Portugal, Puerto Rico, Russia, Spain, Surinam, Turkey, Venezuela, and even more countries. I was surprised that my students from Korea knew "Oh, Susanna!" and that a dentist from Czechoslovakia loved "Clementine." Spanish and Japanese students wanted to sing songs by the Beatles and by Simon and Garfunkel. Songs proved to be a common medium for language-learning among us.

Today, my students from Brazil and from China know "From a Distance" and "We Are the World." Students from Spanish-speaking countries know and love songs by Gloria Estefan and the Miami Sound Machine. All my students learn more English as they sing songs together.

For SING IT! LEARN ENGLISH THROUGH SONG, I picked songs that I like and that students from many different countries asked me to include. I know that these particular songs are good for teaching English.

So, how should you use these songs to learn English? First of all, let's look at the various parts of the SING IT! program, and I will tell you about each part.

Contents of each level

Level One focuses on the Present Tense (verb **to be** & others), Imperative, Future with "going to," and also includes adjectives and adverbs, definite and indefinite articles, colors and numbers, parts of the body, prepositions, and related grammar and vocabulary.

Level Two highlights Present Continuous, Future Tenses with "'ll," "shall" and "will," related grammar and vocabulary, plus a review of the Present Tenses.

Level Three features the Simple Past Tense and Comparisons ("like," "as," comparative and superlative adjectives), related grammar and vocabulary, as well as a review of the Present and Future Tenses.

Level Four focuses on other Past Tenses (Past Continuous, Present Perfect, Past Perfect) and related grammar and vocabulary.

Level Five highlights Conditionals, If, Modals, Wish and more difficult grammar and vocabulary.

Level Six features a grand review of all Verb Tenses, Clauses, Non-standard English, and a Complete Index of the usages in all six levels.

As you can see, the levels progress from elementary to more difficult learning. The various parts of each level, such as the Introductions and Learning Ideas, also progress from easier to more difficult.

Remember, however, that songwriters like to have fun with words, so they do not usually limit themselves to one tense or one particular grammatical point! Because of this, you may find a few difficult parts in the early songs, and some easy parts in the more advanced selections.

Songs

Each song contains many features which are useful for learning: an Introduction, listing of Key Structures, the Music and Song Lyrics, and Learning Ideas to enhance and challenge your comprehension of the language and words of the song.

- The **Introduction** tells you something about the song, the composers, the artists who originally performed it and, often, some related cultural or historical background. The introduction is repeated on the cassette, so you can listen to spoken English to improve your listening skills, and then say it back to see how your speaking compares with the person on the cassette.

- **Key Structures** tell you which structures and usages are important in the song. For each Key Structure, you will see one or more examples as they appear in the song and in the Song Lyrics themselves. By paying attention to this material, you can learn something new or sharpen your knowledge of already-learned structures.

- **Communicative Objectives** let you know different topics that you can practice talking and writing about, and what you can expect to know to do when you complete your study of each song.

- The **Music** and complete **Song Lyrics** invite you to listen actively, look and sing along with the artists. For those of you who read music, we include the first verse and chorus with the written music. Then for your ease in studying, we include the first verse of the songs with the music, followed by the complete lyrics under the written music. If you play guitar or piano, you can follow the notes and chords to accompany the songs.

- **Learning Ideas** are designed especially to add to your fun as you move through each level. These sections have four specific parts:

  - **Vocabulary** so that you can pick out new words and use them.
  - **Questions about the Song** so that you can test your understanding of the song and the lyrics.
  - **Questions for You** to invite you to think of your own ideas and write them down.
  - **Extra Learning** to expand your knowledge and to challenge you to learn even more. Some of these questions may be too difficult for you. If they are, come back to them later when your English is more advanced.

  Some songs also have **Footnotes** which explain difficult material.

Indexes

At the end of the book are four sections which make it easier for you to find things: indexes of songs by Artist, by Genre/Theme, by Grammatical Usage, and by Song Title.

- **Artist Index:** You may want to find a song that Gloria Estefan sings, or that Pete Seeger composed. You can look in the Artist Index for the last name of the artist to see what songs are included. For example, under Estefan, Gloria, you will see "Rhythm Is Gonna Get You," and find that it is on page 50.

- **Genre/Theme Index:** Suppose you want to hear a song about cowboys, or maybe you want your class to talk about peace. You can look in the Genre/Theme Index to see which songs focus on these themes. If you look under Family, you will find two songs, the names of the songs, and what pages they are on.

- **Grammatical Index:** Maybe you want to practice the Future Tense. Look this up in the Grammatical Index. For Future Tense, you will find "Those bones are going to rise again" from the song "Dry Bones," page 46, and other songs which contain the Future Tense.

- **Song Index:** This is the index you will probably use most often, so I put it at the end of the book where you can refer to it easily. Are you looking for the song "Rock My Soul"? Look in this index under "R," and you will see "Rock My Soul" listed and find that it is on page 17.

The Level Six Text/Workbook has a complete index of all six books.

Answer Key

Your Text/Workbook contains an Answer Key if you are using **SING IT! LEARN ENGLISH THROUGH SONG** without a teacher. It provides answers to the specific questions in Learning Ideas.

A final note: You may use **SING IT! LEARN ENGLISH THROUGH SONG** for simple enjoyment and for learning, inside or outside the classroom.

SPECIAL NOTES FOR STUDENTS WITHOUT TEACHERS

If you are not taking English classes now, or do not have your own teacher, you may want to follow these suggestions:

1. Select a specific song.
   The **Table of Contents** and **Indexes** will help you choose a song according to your interest or according to the area of usage you want to practice.
2. On your cassette recorder, play the spoken Introduction to the song.
   Listen *without looking at the words.* Listen, in a relaxed way, but with curiosity to see how much you can understand. This active listening sharpens your discriminatory skills and stretches your learning capacities. Repeat this several times.
3. Now open your Text/Workbook and look at the **Introduction**
   How many words did you hear correctly? Write them down. Which words surprise you? Write them down.
4. Play the Introduction again and silently read along with it.
   Now try saying the words along with the person on the tape.
   Do this as many times as you wish. Each time you do this, you can gain confidence and skill. Listen to the rhythm of the words and try to match it.
5. Look at the **Key Structures** in the Text/Workbook to give yourself a preview of the song.
6. Now close your book and play the song.
   Follow the suggestions for listening that are noted above in 2.
7. Ask yourself:
   What is this song about? What do I understand? Which words or parts don't I understand? Can I understand the unfamiliar words better if I think about the words that come before and after them?
8. Write down words and phrases that you understand.
9. Replay the entire song.
   Ask yourself: Do I understand more of the song now?
10. Play the first phrase.
    Listen to it and repeat it. Do this as often as necessary.
11. Continue in the same way with the other phrases.
    Let yourself breathe and relax as you listen. You may even want to lie on the floor and stretch out, or dance and move as you hear the song.
12. Now open your Text/Workbook again and look at the words as you listen to the complete song.
    How many of them did you guess right? Which ones surprise you?

13. Look at the **Communicative Objectives.**
    If you are studying with someone, look for ways that you can practice each objective, both in conversation and in writing. If you are studying by yourself, create your own ways of practicing and developing each objective. Use your previous notes, your dictionary and your own good instincts to help you.
14. Do the **Vocabulary** exercises in your Text/Workbook.
    Be sure to write down carefully the new words you are learning.
15. Sing the entire song along with the cassette.
    Do this as many times as you wish. You can do one verse at a time, or, if you are in the mood, sing the whole song.
16. Write in the answers to the **Questions about the song.**
    If you are not sure of an answer, go back to the song to look for ideas.
17. Write in the answers to the **Questions for you.** Use your creativity and imagination as you fill in these answers.
18. Study the **Extra Learning** sections and fill in the answers to the exercises.
    You do not need to do all of these exercises at one sitting. Sometimes it helps your learning to take a relaxation break. Walk around and stretch, look out a window, and then simply play the song again for enjoyment. Now go back to finish another part of the Extra Learning sections.
19. Verify your answers to the specific questions by checking with the **Answer Key.** Before looking at the answers, be sure you write down your own responses in your Text/Workbook. Then check them by looking at the Answer Key.

Have fun being your own teacher. See how much you can learn on your own. Give yourself a good grade when you do a particularly successful lesson.

You may enjoy listening to the songs as you take the bus or drive to work or school, as you do things around your home or at the beach, or before you go to bed. The songs slip into your brain unconsciously. Before you know it, you will be humming along, then singing along in English.

ACKNOWLEDGMENTS AND THANKS

I want to thank:

Eric A. Anderson and Bob Briar at Cutler's Records in New Haven, Gordon Emerson, Molly Fleming, John Forster, Jeff Fuller, Cliff Furnald, Sal Libro and Pete Seeger for their musical input and enthusiasm.

Alexis Johnson and all the instructors and students at the International Language Institute of Massachusetts, Inc.; Jan Hortas and instructors and students at Yale English Language Institute; Marian Knight and all at ELS Language Center at Albertus Magnus College in New Haven, Connecticut; Karen Serret of the Bilingual Program in Waterbury, Ct.; Bob Nelson of City College of San Francisco; Lyn Jacob and Jane Larson of the Instituto de Estudios Norteamericanos in Barcelona and all past students and teachers there, especially ex director Bob Ramsey – for helping shape the contents and direction of SING IT! LEARN ENGLISH THROUGH SONG.

Jane Baron Rechtman, Bruce P. Blair, my Bloom family–Paul, Noah, Josh, Miriam and Martha–Jason Bohannon, Larry Cerri, Eric Chen, Maureen E. Daly, Kathy Davis, Joe FitzGerald, Jacqueline Flamm, Ethel Granick, John Holland, Lynn Johnson-Martin, Zarah Johnson-Morris, Sheila Lirio, Marga Mueller, George W. Nowacki, Randi Parker, Dick Payne, Ilana Rubenfeld and my Rubenfeld Synergy friends, Mitsue Sakamoto, Wendy Samberg, Maia Scott, Angelyn Singer, Paul Spector, Jesse Sugarmann, Chris Tolsdorf, Rebecca Totaro, Cheryl R. Wiener, Jianxin Yang, Hongbo Zang–for their ongoing consultation and support.

My editor Louise Jennewine for her thorough dedication and good humor, Janet Gomolson for her unstinting enthusiasm, Fred Perkins for believing in SING IT! way back then and now, and Lowell Britson for stepping in to help us out.

Special thanks to my own Kentucky family and to all the people around the world who have taught me songs and learned songs from me.

Millie Grenough

ACKNOWLEDGMENTS FOR SONGS

We have made every effort to determine the copyright status of the songs included in this book. We wish to thank the publishers of the following songs for permission to reprint their copyrighted material.

"As Tears Go By" by Mick Jagger, Keith Richards and Andrew Loog Oldham. Copyright © 1964 (renewed) Forward Music Ltd., London, England. TRO - Essex Music Inc., New York, controls all publication rights for the USA and Canada. Used by permission.

"Colours" by Donovan Leitch. Copyright © 1965 by Southern Music Publishing Co., Ltd. Assigned to Donovan (Music) Ltd. Administered by Southern Music Publishing Co., Inc. Used by permission.

"Deep in the Heart of Texas" by June Hershey and Don Swander. Copyright © 1941 by Melody Lane Publications, Inc. Copyright renewed. Used by permission.

"Rhythm Is Gonna Get You" by G. Estefan, E. Garcia and M. Lewis. Copyright © 1987 Foreign Imported Productions and Publishing, Inc. International copyright secured. All rights reserved.

"There's a Hole in the Bottom of the Sea" from **The Book of Navy Songs,** copyright © 1955, Joseph W. Crosley and the United States Naval Institute. Used by permission.

"Turn! Turn! Turn! (To Everything There is A Season)" - words from the Book of Ecclesiastes, adaptation and music by Pete Seeger. TRO - copyright © 1962, Melody Trails, Inc., New York, New York. Used by permission.

Our appreciation to the staff of the Archive of Folk Songs of the Library of Congress in Washington, D.C., and the staff of the New Haven Public Library for their assistance. The following songs were adapted from field recordings in the Archive of American Folklore in Washington, D.C., and from other public domain material: "Dry Bones," "He's Got the Whole World," "Michael, Row the Boat Ashore," "Rock My Soul" (new verses by Millie Grenough), "Shalom Chaverim" (English words by Millie Grenough and Neal Rechtman), "Take Me Out to the Ball Game" (words by Jack Norworth, music by Albert von Tilzer), "When the Saints Go Marching In."

COLOURS[1]

Donovan Leitch, a folk singer from Glasgow, Scotland. (UPI/Bettmann)

Donovan Leitch, a folk singer and guitar player from Glasgow, Scotland, made[2] his first record when he was[3] eighteen years old. He composed many songs, including "Mellow Yellow" and "Universal Soldier." In this song he sings of love and nature. He uses the colors yellow and green to paint his picture.
What colors do you use to talk about nature and about the people you love?

KEY STRUCTURES

- **Present Tense**   Yellow **is** the colour

- **Adverb**   I **rarely** use

- **Expressions**   **mm-hmm, uh-huh**

- **Possessive**   my true **love's** hair

- **Reductions**   **mornin', sparklin', feelin', thinkin'**

[1] **colours:** British spelling; in the United States, **color**
[2] **made:** past tense of **make**
[3] **was:** past tense of **is**

COMMUNICATIVE OBJECTIVES

- to describe people
- to talk about colors and various objects
- to express feelings

Colours

Words and music by
DONOVAN

Yel-low is the co-lour of my true love's

hair in the morn-in' When we

rise, in the morn-in'

when we rise. CHORUS: That's the

time, that's the time

I love the best.

SONG LYRICS

1. Yellow **is** the colour of my true **love's** hair in the **mornin'**[4]
   When we **rise,** in the **mornin'** when we **rise.**

   CHORUS: That's[5] the time, that's the time I **love** the best.

2. Green's the color of the **sparklin'**[4] corn in the **mornin'**
   When we **rise,** in the **mornin'** when we **rise:**   CHORUS

3. Mellow **is** the **feelin'**[4] that I get when I **see** her
   Mm-hmm[6] when I **see** her **uh-huh.**[6]   CHORUS

4. Freedom **is** a word I **rarely** use without **thinkin'**[4] mm-hmm
   Without **thinkin' mm-hmm** of the time, of the time, when I've been loved.[7]

LEARNING IDEAS

- *Vocabulary*

  1. In this song, which words are new for you? Write them down. _____

  2. Can you use them in sentences?

  3. What is another way to say "rarely"? (verse 4) _____

---

[4] **mornin', sparklin', feelin', thinkin':** reductions of **morning, sparkling, feeling, thinking**
[5] **That's:** contracted form of **that is**
[6] **mm-hmm, uh-huh:** humming sounds; can also mean "yes"
[7] **I've been loved:** present perfect tense, passive voice. See Level Four for more examples.

4. What is another way to say "rise"? (verses 1 & 2) _____

5. What is another way to say "sparkling"? (verse 2) _____

- *Questions about the song*

    1. What time of day does the singer love the best? _____

    2. What color is his true love's hair? _____

    3. What color is the corn? _____

- *Questions for you*

    1. What colors do you love the best? _____
    _____

    2. How does each of these colors make you feel? _____
    _____

    3. What do you associate with the color green? _____

    4. How do you feel when you see the color purple? _____
    _____

    5. What is another word for "mellow"? _____

    6. What makes you feel mellow? _____

- *Extra learning*

    Possessive

    1. What color is your mother's hair? *Her hair is red.*

    2. What size are your best friend's shoes? _____

    3. What colors are in your country's flag? _____

    Write your own poem/song about:

    1. a friend of yours
    2. your hometown
    3. your country

DEEP IN THE HEART OF TEXAS

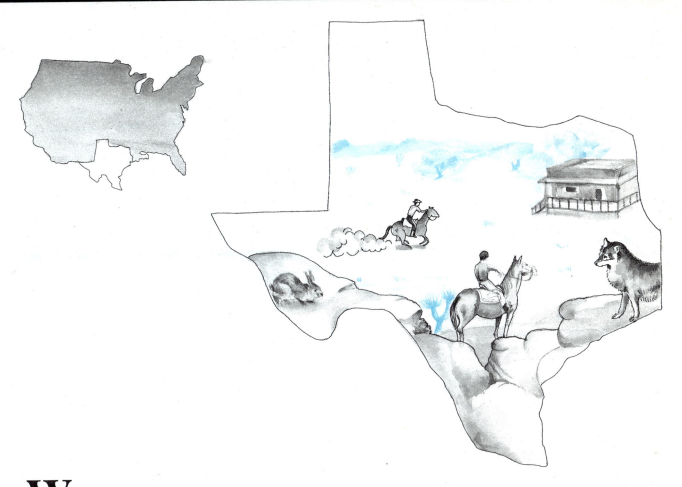

We all have special feelings about our birthplaces. Some of us believe that they are the best places in the world. Many people write poems or songs about their homes and their own people. Some people paint pictures of their birthplaces in their songs.
The person in this songs misses her home state of Texas, the second largest in the U.S.A. She sings about Texas and about the person she loves there.

 KEY STRUCTURES

- **Present Tense**   The stars at night **are** + others

- **Adjectives**   **big** and **bright, wide** and **high**

- **Definite Article**   **the** stars, **the** prairie sky + others

- **"is like"**   the sage in bloom **is like** perfume

- **Prepositions**   **in** the heart, **along** the trail + others

COMMUNICATIVE OBJECTIVES

- to describe your birthplace or hometown
- to talk about cowboys
- to describe things using definite articles and adjectives

Deep In The Heart Of Texas

Words and music by
JUNE HERSHEY and DON SWANDER

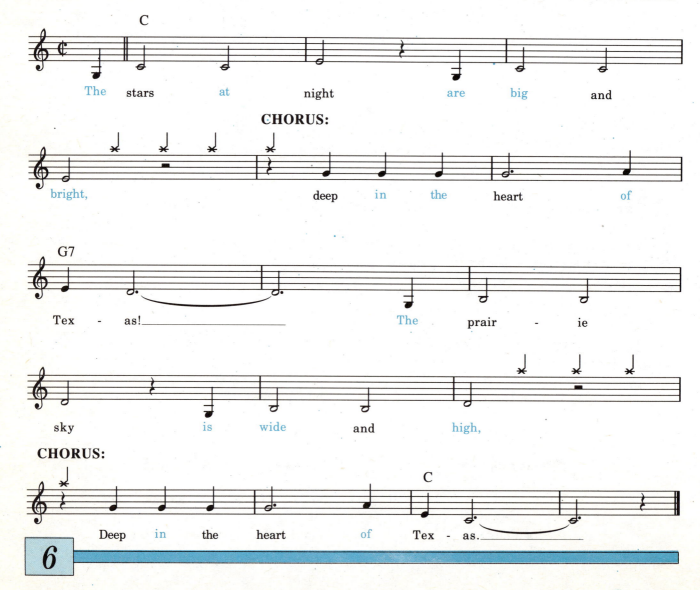

SONG LYRICS

1. The stars at night are big and bright,

    CHORUS: XXXX[1] deep in the heart of Texas!

    The prairie sky is wide and high.   CHORUS

2. The sage in bloom is like perfume,   CHORUS
   Reminds me of the one I love,   CHORUS

3. The coyotes wail along the trail,   CHORUS
   The rabbits rush around the brush,   CHORUS

4. The cowboys cry "Ki-yip-pee-yi,"   CHORUS
   The dogies[2] bawl and bawl and bawl,   CHORUS

LEARNING IDEAS

- *Vocabulary*

    1. In this song, which words are new for you? Write them down. _____

    2. Can you use them in sentences?

    3. What is another way to say "bawl"? _____

- *Questions about the song*

    1. What is the sage in bloom like? _____

    2. What do the coyotes do? _____
    _____

    3. What do the rabbits do? _____

    4. What do you think "Ki-yip-pee-yi" means? _____

    5. Is it a happy or a sad sound? _____

---

[1] **X:** clap your hands once each time you see an "X."
[2] **dogies:** baby cows without mothers

- *Questions for you*

    1. Do you have cowboys or people like them in your country? _____
    2. What sounds do they make? _____
    3. How do you say them? _____

- *Extra learning*

    Adjectives

    Find words that mean the opposite:

    1. big _____*little*_____   4. bright _____
    2. high _____   5. wide _____
    3. rush _____   6. love _____

    "is like _____"

    Make up your own endings:

    1. The sage in bloom is like _____
    2. The sun at dawn is like _____
    3. The food at home is like _____
    4. The rivers in my country are like _____

    "Remind me of" + noun; "Remind me to" + verb

    Make up your own endings:

    1. This song reminds me of _____
    2. My teacher always reminds me to _____

    Can you write a version of this song about your birthplace?

MICHAEL, ROW THE BOAT ASHORE

This is a work song sung[1] by United States slaves in the nineteenth century. The singers work in this difficult world. As they row their masters' boats, they dream of happiness in the next world, on the other side of the Jordan River. The Jordan is the river that was[2] the beginning of the Promised Land for the Israelite people many centuries earlier.

[1] **sung:** past participle of **sing**, passive voice.
[2] **was:** past tense of **is**

KEY STRUCTURES

- **Imperative**
  - Affirmative — Michael, **row** the boat + others
  - Negative — **Don't** forget the poor

- **Phrasal Verb** — **wipe away** my pain

- **Definite Article** — **the** boat + others
  Indefinite Article — **a** helping hand

- **Gerund as Adjective** — **helping** hand

- **Times of day** — blow it **night** and blow it **morn**[3]

COMMUNICATIVE OBJECTIVES

- to talk about family members

- to give orders and commands

- to describe what you do in the morning and at night

Michael, Row The Boat Ashore

Mi-chael, row____ the boat a-shore, hal-le-lu-jah! Mi-chael row the boat a-shore, hal-le-lu-jah!

[3] **morn**: a shortened form of morning

10

SONG LYRICS

1. Michael, row the boat ashore, hallelujah[4]   REPEAT

2. Gabriel[5], blow the trumpet horn, hallelujah!
   Blow it night and blow it morn, hallelujah!

3. Brother, lend a helping hand, hallelujah!   REPEAT

4. Sister, help to hold the sail, hallelujah!   REPEAT

5. Mother, wait for me over there, hallelujah!
   Wipe away my pain and care, hallelujah!

6. Michael, haul the boat ashore, hallelujah!
   Take the rich and don't[6] forget the poor, hallelujah!

7. Trumpet, sound the jubilee[7], hallelujah!
   Trumpet, sound for you and me, hallelujah!

 ## LEARNING IDEAS

- *Vocabulary*

   1. In this song, which words are new for you? Write them down.
      _____

   2. Can you use them in sentences?

   3. What is another way to say "wipe away"? (verse 5) _____

   4. What is another way to say "haul"? (verse 6) _____

- *Questions about the song*

   1. What does Gabriel blow? _____

   2. When does he blow it? _____

---

[4] **hallelujah:** Hebrew word meaning "Praise the Lord"
[5] **Gabriel:** an archangel
[6] **don't:** contracted form of **do not**
[7] **jubilee:** time of celebration

3. What does the singer ask his brother to do? _____

4. What two things does he ask his mother to do? _____

- **Questions for you**

    1. Do you have any brothers? _____

       How many? _____

       Are they older or younger than you? _____

    2. Do you have any sisters? _____

       Do you ever ask your sisters to do anything for you? _____

    3. What are two things your mother asks you to do for her? _____
       _____

- **Extra learning**

    ### Times of day

    1. What are two things you do in the morning? _____
       _____

    2. Describe two things you do at night. _____
       _____

    ### Imperatives

    Compose your own endings for these imperatives:

    1. Maria, wait for *me by the drugstore.*_____.

    2. Tom, take _____.

    3. Mother, _____.

    ### Verbs of action

    There are ten verbs in this song. Can you dramatize them?
    Choose three of the verbs and act them out for your classmates.

TAKE ME OUT TO THE BALL GAME

This is the song for baseball, a favorite sport in Costa Rica, Japan, Mexico, Nicaragua, Panama, Puerto Rico, the United States, and many other countries. People who like a sport a lot are called "fans." When baseball fans sing this song, they are cheering for their home team.

KEY STRUCTURES

- Imperative — Take me out to the ball game + others

- Present Tense
    - Contracted form — it's[1] one, two, three strikes, you're[2] out
    - Negative — I don't[3] care

- Phrasal Verbs — take me out, never get back

- Adverb — I never get back

- Numbers — one, two, three strikes

[1] it's: contracted form of it is
[2] you're: contracted form of you are
[3] don't: contracted form of do not

COMMUNICATIVE OBJECTIVES

- to discuss baseball and your favorite players
- to state your preferences in food and drink
- to explain your likes and dislikes

Take Me Out To The Ball Game

Words by Jack Norworth
Music by Albert von Tilzer

CHORUS:

1. Take me out to the ball game. Take me

out with the crowd. Buy me some pea-nuts and

crack-er jack. I don't care if I nev-er get

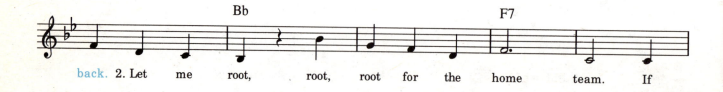
back. 2. Let me root, root, root for the home team. If

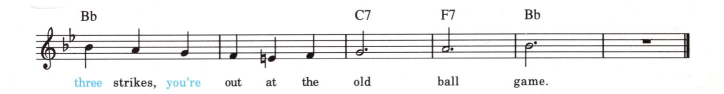

 ## SONG LYRICS

1. **Take** me out to the ball game. **Take** me out with the crowd.
   Buy me some peanuts and crackerjack.
   I **don't** care if **I never get back**.[4]

2. Let me root, root, root for the home team.
   If they **don't** win, it's a shame.
   For it's **one, two, three** strikes, **you're** out at the old ball game.

   REPEAT entire song.

 ## LEARNING IDEAS

- *Vocabulary*

   1. In this song, which words are new for you? Write them down.
      _____

   2. Can you use them in sentences?
   3. What is another way to say "get back"? _____
   4. What is another way to say "root"? _____

[4] **Never get back:** non-standard English. Standard English: ever get back

- *Questions about the song*

    1. Where do the singers want to go? _____
    2. What kinds of food do they want? _____
    3. Who do they want to cheer for? _____
    4. How many strikes make an out? _____

- *Questions for you*

    1. Do you like to play baseball? _____
    2. What do you like about baseball? _____
    3. What don't you like about baseball? _____
    4. Does your home city have a baseball team? _____
    5. If so, what is the name of the team? _____
    6. Who are your two favorite baseball players? _____ and _____
    7. Give reasons why you like each one. _____
    8. What kinds of food do you like to eat at a ball game? _____
    9. What do you like to drink? _____

- *Extra learning*

    ### Imperatives

    Imagine that you have a five-year-old sister and that she is asking you to do things for her. Complete these sentences as a five-year-old:

    1. Take me _to the park with you._ _____
    2. Buy me some _____
    3. Draw me a picture of _____

ROCK MY SOUL

In this song, the singer calls out to Abraham, a great hero of the Bible. The "bosom" of Abraham represents safety, freedom, love, and never-ending joy for anyone in trouble.
For other traditional African-American songs in this book, see "Dry Bones," p. 46, "He's Got the Whole World," p. 34, and "Michael, Row the Boat Ashore," p. 9.

 ## KEY STRUCTURES

- **Imperative**   Rock my soul

- **Present Tense**   I'm[1] in the bosom + others

---
[1] **I'm:** contracted form of **I am**

- **Modals**
  - Affirmative — I **can feel** the light
  - Negative — you **can't**[2] get over it + others

- **Adjectives** — **high, low, dark** + others

- **Gerunds as Adjectives** — **towering** man, light **shining**

- **"Oh" as Exclamation** — **Oh,** rock my soul!

- **Prepositions** — **over, under** + others

- **So + Adjective** — **so high, so wide** + others

COMMUNICATIVE OBJECTIVES

- to talk about heroes and heroines

- to identify places

- to create rhymes

Rock My Soul

CHORUS:

Rock__ my soul__ in the bo-som of A - bra - ham.

Rock my soul__ in the bo-som of A - braham. Rock__ my soul__ in the

---

[2]**can't**: contracted form of **can not**

 SONG LYRICS

CHORUS: **Rock**[3] **my soul in** the bosom of Abraham.   REPEAT three times

Oh, rock my soul!
So high you can't get over it, so low you can't get under it,
So wide you can't get around it. Oh, rock my soul!

[3] **Rock:** pronounced "Rock-a" in this song to add rhythm

1. **I'm in** the bosom of Abraham. **Oh, rock** my soul!
   I'm safe **in** the shadow **of** the **towering** man. **Oh, rock** my soul!   CHORUS

2. His bosom is **dark** and **deep** and **wide**. **Oh, rock** my soul!
   And I **can feel** the light **shining from** inside. **Oh, rock** my soul!   CHORUS

LEARNING IDEAS

- *Vocabulary*

   1. In this song, which words are new for you? Write them down.
      _____

   2. Can you use them in sentences?

- *Questions about the song*

   1. Where does the singer want his soul to be? _____

   2. Find three adjectives to describe the bosom of Abraham. _____
      _____

   3. What can the singer feel (verse 2)? _____

- *Questions for you*

   1. Who are two of your favorite heroes or heroines?
      _____

   2. Give two reasons why you like each one.
      _____

   3. Where are two places that you feel safe? _____
      _____

- **Extra Learning**

   So + adjective

   Finish these sentences:

   1. _That hill_ is so high that I can't _climb it_.

   2. _____ is so dark that I can't _____.

   3. _____ is so difficult that Ana and Peter can't _____.

   Adjectives

   Find words that mean the opposite of these adjectives:

   1. high _low_   4. safe _____

   2. wide _____   5. deep _____

   3. dark _____

   Prepositions

   What are the opposites of these prepositions?

   1. over _under_   3. in _____

   2. behind _____

   Write sentences using these prepositions.

   Rhymes

   Rhymes are words that sound the same. Can you find words to rhyme with the following words? See if you can find more than one word for each.

   1. deep   _sleep_   _leap_

   2. light   _____   _____

   3. strong _____   _____

   4. wide   _____   _____

THERE'S A HOLE

Imagination is a wonderful thing. It can help you travel through clouds and see things on the moon, or dive through miles of water and see things on the bottom of the ocean. In this song the singer sees many things on a piece of a tree in the water.

 KEY STRUCTURES

- **Present Tense**   **There's** a hole + others

- **Prepositions**   bump **on** the log **in** the hole **in** the bottom **of** the sea

- **There is**   **There's** a hole + others

22

COMMUNICATIVE OBJECTIVES

- to talk about many objects at the same time

- to tell what is here and to state its exact location

There's A Hole

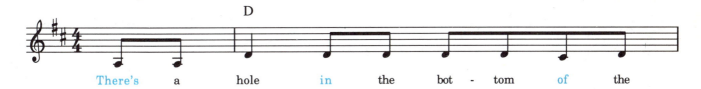

There's a hole in the bot-tom of the

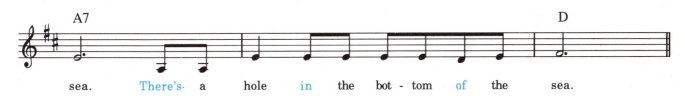

sea. There's a hole in the bot-tom of the sea.

CHORUS:

There's a hole, there's a hole, there's a

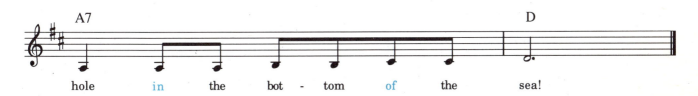

hole in the bot-tom of the sea!

SONG LYRICS

1. **There's** a hole **in** the bottom **of** the sea.   **REPEAT**

   CHORUS: **There's** a hole, **there's** a hole,
   There's a hole **in** the bottom **of** the sea!

2. There's a log in the hole in the bottom of the sea. REPEAT + CHORUS

3. There's a bump on the log in the hole in the bottom of the sea. REPEAT + CHORUS

4. There's a frog on the bump on the log
   in the hole in the bottom of the sea. REPEAT + CHORUS

5. There's a fly on the frog on the bump on the log
   in the hole in the bottom of the sea. REPEAT + CHORUS

6. There's a flea on the fly on the frog on the bump
   on the log in the hole in the bottom of the sea. REPEAT + CHORUS

 ## LEARNING IDEAS

- *Vocabulary*

    1. In this song, which words are new for you? Write them down.
    _____

    2. Can you use them in sentences?

    3. What is another way to say "sea"? _____

- *Questions about the song*

    1. Where is there a hole? _____
    2. What is in the hole? _____
    3. What is on the log? _____
    4. What is on the frog? _____

- *Questions for you*

    1. Is there a sea near your city? _____
    2. If so, what is the name of the sea? _____
    3. Name two things that are on the bottom of the sea. _____
    _____

- *Extra learning*

   There's a:

   Answer yes or no to the following:

   1. There's a French teacher in this room. *No, there's an English teacher in this room.*
   2. There's a hole in the floor. _____
   3. There's a cat on my desk. _____
   4. There's a pencil in my hand. _____

   Prepositions

   Look around your classroom and complete these sentences.

   1. There's a ___*clock*___ on the wall.
   2. There are _____ students in the room.
   3. _____ are under my desk.
   4. _____ is in front of me.
   5. _____ is behind me.
   6. _____ is beside me.

TURN! TURN! TURN!

Pete Seeger sings to people in New York City.   (UPI/Bettmann)

Much of the wisdom in United States folk songs comes from the Bible. In this song, the songwriter Pete Seeger takes his lyrics from the Book of Ecclesiastes in the Bible. He sings about the changing seasons in human life.

For other songs by Pete Seeger, see "Where Have All the Flowers Gone?" in Level Four and "If I Had a Hammer" in Level Five.

KEY STRUCTURES

- **Imperative**   Turn!

- **Phrasal Verbs**   build up, break down + others

- **There is**   There is a season

- **"too" + Adjective**   it's not too late

COMMUNICATIVE OBJECTIVES

- to find synonyms (words that mean the same thing) and antonyms (opposites)
- to describe excess using "too"
- to talk about seasons and months of the year

Turn! Turn! Turn!

Words from the Book of Eclesiastes
Adaptation and music by Peter Seeger

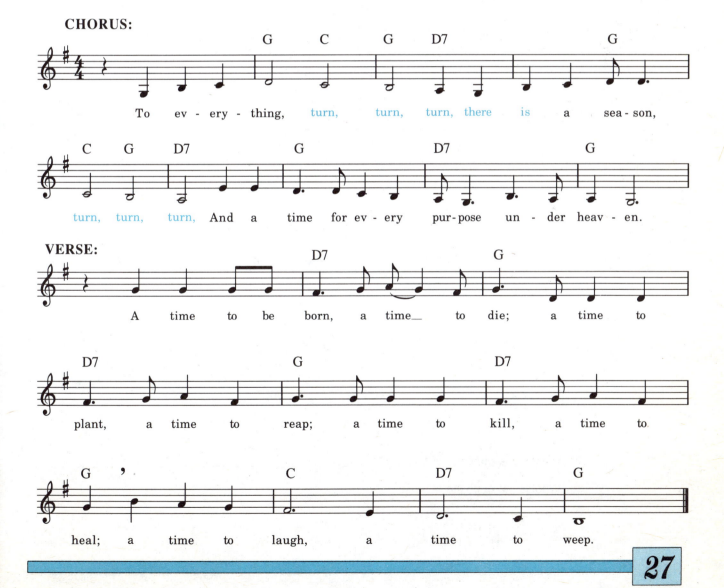

SONG LYRICS

CHORUS: To everything, turn, turn, turn, there is a season, turn, turn, turn,
And a time for every purpose under heaven.

1. A time to be born, a time to die; a time to plant, a time to reap;
   A time to kill, a time to heal; a time to laugh, a time to weep.   CHORUS

2. A time to build up, a time to break down; a time to dance, a time to mourn;
   A time to cast away stones, a time to gather stones together.   CHORUS

3. A time of war, a time of peace; a time of love, a time of hate;
   A time you may embrace, a time to refrain from embracing.   CHORUS

4. A time to gain, a time to lose; a time to rend, a time to sew;
   A time of love, a time of hate; a time of peace--I swear it's not too late.

LEARNING IDEAS

- *Vocabulary*

    1. In this song, which words are new for you? Write them down.
       _____

    2. Can you use them in sentences?

    3. What is another word for "weep"? _____

    4. What is another word for "reap"? _____

- *Questions about the song*

    1. What is the opposite of "to be born"? _____

    2. What is the opposite of "build up"? _____

    3. What is the opposite of "love"? _____

- *Questions for you*

    1. Name two crops that grow in your country. _____
    _____

    2. For each crop, what month is the time to plant? _____
    _____

    3. What month is the time to reap? _____
    _____

- *Extra Learning*

    ### Action Verbs

    There are more than ten action verbs in this song. Write down five of the verbs. Then pantomime (dramatize) one verb at a time and ask your classmates to guess the verb.

    _____
    _____
    _____

    ### Opposites

    Write the opposite of each of these words:

    1. laugh — *weep or cry*
    2. war — _____
    3. mourn — _____
    4. cast away — _____

    ### Too + Adjective

    Complete these sentences:

    1. I am too tired to *play my guitar.*
    2. Freddy and Johnny are too young to _____.
    3. That _____ is too expensive.
    4. That _____ is too loud.

SHALOM CHAVERIM[1] (We Wish You Peace)

There are many ways to say "peace." In Portuguese and Spanish, it is *paz*. In Arabic, it is *salaam*; in French, *paix*. in Japanese, *heiwa*. In Hebrew, *shalom* can mean "peace," " good–bye", and "hello."
The persons in this old Israeli song are saying "good-bye" and wishing "peace" to everyone in the family. You may sing this song as a round: one group begins, and then the next group starts after the first group sings the words "We wish you peace for all of your kin".

[1] **Shalom Chaverim:** Hebrew for "Peace to you, my friends"

KEY STRUCTURES

- **Present Tense**   We **wish** you peace + others
- **Relatives**   all of your **kin**
- **Till = until**   **till** we meet again

COMMUNICATIVE OBJECTIVES

- to explore ways to say words in different languages
- to identify relatives (aunts, uncles, cousins) and talk about them
- to discuss songs from your own country

Shalom Chaverim

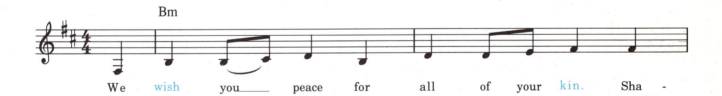

We **wish** you peace for all of your **kin.** Sha-

lom, sha - lom. We **sing** this song **till**

we **meet** a-gain. Sha-lom, sha - lom.

SONG LYRICS[2]

We **wish** you peace for all of your **kin**. Shalom, shalom.

We **sing** this song **till** we **meet** again. Shalom, shalom.　　　REPEAT entire song.

LEARNING IDEAS

- *Vocabulary*

    1. In this song, which words are new for you? Write them down.
    _____

    2. Can you use them in sentences?

    3. What is another way to say "kin"? _____

- *Questions about the song*

    1. What is the Hebrew word for "peace"? _____

    2. Are the people in this song saying "hello" or "good-bye"? _____

    3. Till when are the people in this song singing? _____

- *Questions for you*

    1. Do you know a song from your country that says "good-bye"? _____

        What is the name of the song? _____

        Is it a happy or sad song? _____

    2. Do you know a song that wishes "peace"? _____

        What is the name of the song? _____

        When do people sing the song? _____

[2] **The song lyrics in Hebrew are:** *Shalom chaverim, shalom chaverim, shalom, shalom,
　　Le hit ra-ot, le hit ra-ot, shalom, shalom.*

- *Extra Learning*

Relatives (kin)

1. Do you have many relatives? _____
2. How many aunts do you have? _____
3. What are their names? _____
4. How many uncles? _____
5. What are their names? _____
6. Do you have more cousins on your mother's side or on your father's side? _____
7. How many first cousins do you have on each side? _____
8. Are your relatives all living in one country? _____
9. If not, where do they live? _____

Till = until

Complete these sentences:

1. Mary Ann is studying English till *Bob comes home.*
2. This class lasts till _____
3. Bob is waiting till _____

HE'S GOT[1] THE WHOLE WORLD

Artists with passion and persistence can create incredible beauty out of intense suffering. The songs created by the African-American slaves are such works of art. The song writers and singers carried these beautiful songs from plantation[2] to plantation to give them hope even in the darkest of times. In this song, the singer knows that he is safe because God has the whole world in his hands.

For other traditional African-American songs in this book, see "Dry Bones," p. 46, Michael, Row the Boat Ashore," p. 9, and "Rock My Soul," p. 17.

[1] **He's got:** contracted form of **He has got**
[2] **plantation:** a large farm worked by resident laborers

KEY STRUCTURES

- **"'s got" = has**   He**'s got** the whole world

- **Adjectives**   the **whole** world, the **little-bitty** baby

COMMUNICATIVE OBJECTIVES

- to talk about traditional African-American songs

- to identify what you and others have

He's Got The Whole World

He's got the whole world in his hands. He's got the

whole wide world in his hands. He's got the whole world

CHORUS:

in his hands. He's got the whole world in his hands.

35

SONG LYRICS

1. He's got the whole world in his hands.
   He's got the whole wide world in his hands.
   He's got the whole world in his hands.

   CHORUS: He's got the whole world in his hands.

2. He's got you and me, brother, in his hands.   REPEAT two times.
   CHORUS

3. He's got the little-bitty[3] baby in his hands.   REPEAT two times.
   CHORUS

4. He's got all of us here in his hands.   REPEAT two times.
   CHORUS

LEARNING IDEAS

- *Vocabulary*

   1. In this song, which words are new for you? Write them down.
   _____

   2. Can you use them in sentences?

- *Questions about the song*

   1. Who is "He" in this song? _____

   2. What are the four things He has in his hands? _____
   _____
   _____

---

[3] **little-bitty:** adjective meaning **very little**

- **Questions for you**

    1. What do you have in your hands right now? _____
    2. What does your teacher have in his/her hands? _____
    3. Do you have anything in your pockets? _____
       If so, what? _____

- **Extra Learning**

    "'s got = has

    Practice using "got" in these questions.
    Then write two answers for each question.

    1. What has Barbara got in her hand?
       She's got *a book about rock groups in her hand.*
       She has _____
    2. What has Tony got in his pocket?
       He's got _____
       He has _____

    Make up your own verses and sing them with your classmates.

    1. He's got (name of your city) _____
    2. He's got (names of some of your classmates) _____
    3. He's **got** (name of your country) _____
    4. He's got (name of your family) _____

AS TEARS GO BY

The Rolling Stones--"the greatest rock-and-roll band in the world." (The Bettmann Archive)

"As Tears Go By" is one of the calmer songs sung[1] by the British group, the Rolling Stones. In the 1960s, the Rolling Stones billed themselves as "the greatest rock-and-roll band in the world." The two main members of the group, Mick Jagger and Keith Richards, were[2] friends in primary school. When they met[3] later in London, they formed a quintet and named it "The Rolling Stones" after a song by the African-American blues singer, Muddy Waters.

Three decades later, with some changes in musicians, the Rolling Stones continue to sing, make music and put on shows. Other songs by the Stones include "I Can't[4] Get No Satisfaction", "Ruby Tuesday" and "Honky Tonk Women".

KEY STRUCTURES

- **Present Tense** — I *sit* and *watch* + others

- **Modals**
  - Affirmative — I *can* see
  - Negative — My riches *can't* buy

- **"used to" + Verb** — things I *used to do*

- **Gerunds as Adjectives** — *smiling* faces, rain *falling* on the ground

- **Reductions** — *can't*[4] buy *ev'rything, doin'*[5] things

---

[1] **sung:** past participle of **sing**, passive voice. See Level Four for more examples.
[2] **were:** past tense of **are**
[3] **met:** past tense of **meet**
[4] **can't:** contracted form of **can not**
[5] **ev'rything** and **doin':** reduction of **doing** and **everything**

COMMUNICATIVE OBJECTIVES

- to talk about what people are doing now
- to discuss things you usually do and when you do them (times of day)
- to describe things you used to do (in the past)

As Tears Go By

Words and music by
MICK JAGGER, KEITH RICHARDS
and ANDREW LOOG OLDHAM

SONG LYRICS

1. It **is** the evening of the day, I **sit** and **watch** the children play.
   Smiling faces I **can see** but not for me. I **sit** and **watch** as tears go by.

2. My riches **can't** buy **ev'rything**. I **want** to hear the children **sing**.
   All I **hear** is the sound of rain **falling** on the ground. I **sit** and **watch** as tears go by.

3. (Instrumental)
   Doin' things I **used to do**, they **think** are new, I **sit** and **watch** as tears go by.
   Mmm.

LEARNING IDEAS

- *Vocabulary*

1. In this song, which words are new for you? Write them down.

   _____

2. Can you use them in sentences?

- **Questions about the song**

    1. What is the person in the song doing? _____
    2. Where do you think he is sitting? _____
    3. How old do you think he is? _____
    4. What does he want to hear? _____

- **Questions for you**

    1. What do you usually do in the evening? _____
    _____
    2. What does the line "My riches can't buy ev'rything" mean to you? _____

- **Extra Learning**

    Modals

    1. What can you see from where you are now? *I can see my friend Gonzalo's house from here.*
    2. What can't you see? _____

    "Used to" + Verb; still

    1. Name two games you used to play five years ago. *I used to play nintendo and soccer five years ago.*
    2. Do you still play these games? _____
    3. What are two foods you used to like to eat as a child? _____
    _____
    4. Do you still like them? _____

    Gerunds

    Compose endings using gerunds such as "falling".

    1. In wintertime, I can see snow falling *on the mountains.*
    2. In the evening I see moonlight _____
    3. In the morning I hear birds _____
    4. At suppertime I can watch children _____

WHEN THE SAINTS GO MARCHING IN

Louis Armstrong, the great singer and trumpet player. (UPI/Bettmann)

This song was[1] a camp meeting[2] hymn in the late 1800s. Later, it was a religious revival tune, and then it became[3] a New Orleans jazz number in the early 1900s. Now, it is an international favorite. The singer and trumpeter, Louis Armstrong, helped make this song popular.

See "What a Wonderful World" in Level Three for another song made famous by Louis Armstrong.

[1] **was:** past tense of **is**
[2] **camp meeting:** outdoor church service
[3] **became:** past tense of **become**

KEY STRUCTURES

- **Present Tense**   sun refuses to shine

- **Phrasal Verbs**   when the moon goes down
  the saints go marching in

- **Verb + to + Verb**   I want to be in that number

COMMUNICATIVE OBJECTIVES

- to identify who is doing what

- to talk about refusing to do something

- to say what you want to do and what you like to do

- to describe days of celebration

When The Saints Go Marching In

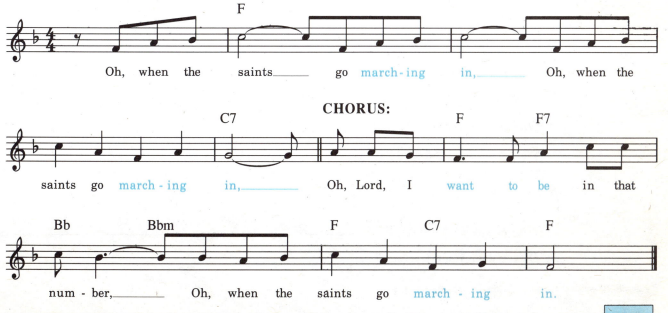

SONG LYRICS

1. Oh, when the saints go marching in,   REPEAT

    CHORUS: Oh, Lord, I want to be in that number,
    Oh, when the saints go marching in.

2. Oh, when the sun refuses to shine,   REPEAT + CHORUS

3. Oh, when the moon goes down in blood,   REPEAT + CHORUS

4. Oh, when old Gabriel blows his horn,   REPEAT + CHORUS

5. Oh, on that jubilation[4] day,   REPEAT + CHORUS

6. Oh, when the saints go marching in,   REPEAT + CHORUS

LEARNING IDEAS

- *Vocabulary*

    1. In this song, which words are new for you? Write them down.
    _____

    2. Can you use them in sentences?

- *Questions about the song*

    1. Who blows the horn? _____
    2. What refuses to shine? _____
    3. Who goes marching in? _____
    4. What goes down in blood? _____

- *Questions for you*

    1. Who do you think the saints are? _____
    2. Do you think you are a saint? _____

[4] **jubilation: similar to jubilee; means a celebration of joy**

3. Do you know someone who blows a horn? _____
4. What kind of horn does she/he blow? _____

- *Extra Learning*

Present Tense

Complete these sentences using the verb "refuse:"

1. My dog always *refuses to play with my cat.*
2. Mr. and Mrs. Nelson _____
3. I _____
4. We _____

Verb + to + Verb

Answer these questions:

1. Do you want to study French next year? *No, I want to study English and Russian.*
2. Does Ms. Jones want to vacation in Colombia? _____
3. Do Mr. and Mrs. Nakamura have to travel to London? _____
4. Does your little sister like to speak English with you? _____
5. How many times a day do you need to eat? _____

Composition

1. What is your favorite day of celebration? _____
   Write down three things you like to do on that day. _____
   _____
   _____

2. Write your own verse to this song and teach it to your classmates as verse 7.

DRY BONES

This traditional African-American song tells about a resurrection when all the dead bodies of the good people are going to live again. You can use this song to learn the names of the parts of the body.
For other traditional African-American songs in this book, see "Rock My Soul," p. 17, "He's Got the Whole World," p. 34, and "Michael, Row the Boat Ashore," p. 9.

KEY STRUCTURES

- **Future with "going to"** those bones are going to rise again

- **Imperative** hear the word of the Lord!

- **Parts of the Body** toe bone, heel bone + others

COMMUNICATIVE OBJECTIVES

- to identify various parts of the body

- to talk about what you are going to do

- to create activities to practice new knowledge

Dry Bones

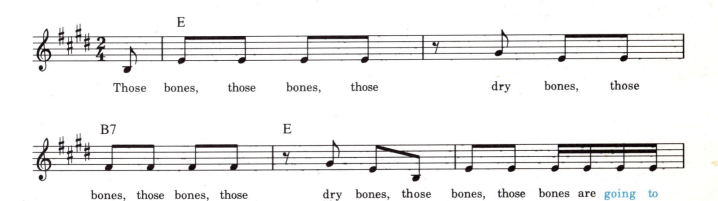

SONG LYRICS

CHORUS: Those bones, those bones, those dry bones, REPEAT
Those bones, those bones are going to rise again.

Now, hear the word of the Lord!

1. The toe bone's[1] connected to the foot bone.
   The foot bone's connected to the heel bone.
   The heel bone's connected to the ankle bone.
   Now, hear the word of the Lord! CHORUS

2. The ankle bone's connected to the leg bone.
   The leg bone's connected to the knee bone.
   The knee bone's connected to the thigh bone.
   Now, hear the word of the Lord! CHORUS

3. The thigh bone's connected to the back bone.
   The back bone's connected to the neck bone.
   The neck bone's connected to the head bone.
   Now, hear the word of the Lord! CHORUS

LEARNING IDEAS

- *Vocabulary*

   1. In this song, which words are new for you? Write them down.
   _____

   2. Can you use them in sentences?

- *Questions about the song*

   1. There are ten bones in this song. Can you find all ten? _____
   _____

   2. Draw a picture of a person. Draw an arrow to each bone and write the correct name.

[1] bone's: contracted form of bone is

- *Questions for you*

    1. Do you have strong bones or weak bones? _____
    2. Do you have any broken bones? If so, which one(s)? _____
    3. When you grow up, do you want to be a doctor? _____
        A nurse? _____ A veterinarian? _____
        Explain why or why not. _____
        _____
        _____

- *Extra Learning*

    Future with "going to"

    1. What time are you going to get up tomorrow? *I am going to get up at 7:00.*
    2. What are you going to eat for breakfast? _____
        _____
    3. When are you going to leave for school? _____
        _____
    4. What are you going to study in class? _____
        _____

    Parts of the body activities

    1. Can you sing this song in reverse? Begin at your head and go down to your toe.
    2. Draw a skeleton and add names of more parts: arms, elbows, hands, fingers, eyes, nose, etc.
    3. Play a quick-response game. Say "Touch your knee" and see how quickly your classmate can do it. Then go to another body part. Make it more difficult by saying "Touch your knee with your elbow," etc.
    4. Practice "right" and "left." Play the quick-response game: "Touch your left ear," etc.

RHYTHM IS GONNA[1] GET YOU

Gloria Estefan, international singer and songwriter. (UPI/Bettmann)

As a teenager, Cuban-born Emilio Estefan organized a small band called the Miami Latin Boys. About the same time, Gloria Fajardo, another Cuban-born Miami teenager, put[2] a band together with some friends. Some months later Gloria attended a friend's wedding where the Miami Latin Boys were playing.[3] Emilio invited Gloria to sing a few songs with the group. Then, Emilio asked her to join the group as a vocalist. About a year later, Gloria and Emilio married.
Gloria Estefan and the Miami Sound Machine are one of the many Latin groups that enrich the world musical scene. They make recordings in Spanish and English.

[1] **Gonna:** reduction of **going to**
[2] **put:** irregular past tense of **put.** See Level Three for more songs with past tenses.
[3] **were playing:** past continuous tense of **play.** See Level Four for more songs with past continuous verbs.

KEY STRUCTURES

- **Future with "going to"**   Rhythm is **gonna** get you
- **Imperative**   **Throw** the covers on your head
- **Phrasal Verb**   **turn off** all the lights
- **Non-standard English**
  pretend like you are dead   pretend as if... or pretend that
  it don't matter   it doesn't matter
- **Reductions**   Rhythm is **gonna** get you
                                  No clue **'bout**[4]

COMMUNICATIVE OBJECTIVES

- to discuss music and your relationship to it
- to identify things that you can "turn off" and "turn on"
- to create a publicity story about what you are going to do

Rhythm Is Gonna Get You

Words and music by
GLORIA ESTEFAN
and ENRIQUE GARCIA

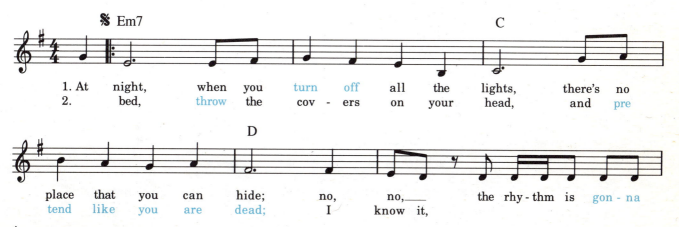

1. At night, when you turn off all the lights, there's no place that you can hide; no, no, the rhythm is gonna
2. bed, throw the covers on your head, and pretend like you are dead; I know it,

[4] **bout**: reduction of **about**

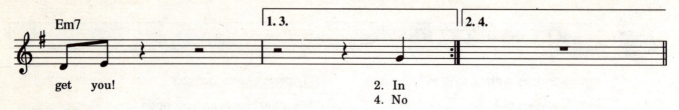

 SONG LYRICS

1. At night, when you **turn off** all the lights, there's no place that you can hide; no, no,
   The rhythm is **gonna** get you!

2. In bed, **throw** the covers on your head, and **pretend like** you are dead;
   I know it, the rhythm is **gonna** get you!

       CHORUS: Rhythm is **gonna** get you,   REPEAT three times
                       Rhythm is **gonna** get you tonight.

3. No way, you can fight it every day. It **don't matter** what you say; you know it,
   The rhythm is **gonna** get you!

4. No clue **'bout** what's happening to you, and before this night is through; ooh baby,
   The rhythm is **gonna** get you!   CHORUS

LEARNING IDEAS

- *Vocabulary*

    1. In this song, which words are new for you? Write them down.
    _____

    2. Can you use them in sentences?

    3. What are other ways to say "no way" and "no clue"? _____
    _____

- *Questions about the song*

    1. Do you think the mood of this song is happy or sad? _____

        Give a good reason for your answer. _____

    2. What is one place where the person in the song tries to hide? _____

- *Questions for you*

    1. What kinds of music appeal to you the most? _____
    _____

    2. When are you going to hear some live music? _____

    3. Do you play any instruments? If so, which ones? _____

        Name two things you like about playing them. _____
    _____
    _____

- *Extra Learning*

    Imperatives

    Think of three ways to "pretend to be dead" and write them in the imperative.

    1. *Lie down and be still.* _____

    2. _____

    3. _____

53

Phrasal Verbs

What are three things you can "turn off"?

1. *I can turn off the radio.*
2. _____
3. _____

What are three things you can "turn on"?

1. *I can turn on my computer.*
2. _____
3. _____

Future with "going to"

Pretend that you are a member of the musical group with Gloria Estefan and the Miami Sound Machine. Write a magazine story about your next tour, using "going to" as much as possible.

My name is...
_____
_____
_____
_____
_____
_____
_____

ARTIST INDEX

Use this index to find a song by a particular composer, instrumental musician or singer.

Armstrong, Louis (singer and instrumentalist)
"When the Saints Go Marching In," 42

Donovan (Leitch, Donovan) (composer and singer)
"Colours," 1

Estefan, Gloria (composer and singer)
"Rhythm Is Gonna Get You," 50

Jagger, Mick (composer and singer)
"As Tears Go By," 38

Leitch, Donovan (Donovan) (composer and singer)
"Colours," 1

Miami Sound Machine (group)
"Rhythm Is Gonna Get You," 50

Richard, Keith (composer and musician)
"As Tears Go By," 38

Rolling Stones, The (group)
"As Tears Go By," 38

Seeger, Pete (composer and singer)
"Turn! Turn! Turn!," 26

GENRE/THEME INDEX

Use this index to find songs with a particular theme.

African-American, traditional
"Dry Bones," 46
"He's Got the Whole World," 34
"Michael, Row the Boat Ashore," 9
"Rock My Soul," 17

Baseball
"Take Me Out to the Ball Game," 13

Bible
"Rock My Soul," 17
"Turn! Turn! Turn!," 26

Birthplace
"Deep in the Heart of Texas," 5

Body
"Dry Bones," 46

Celebration
"Michael, Row the Boat Ashore," 9
"When the Saints Go Marching In," 42

Children
"As Tears Go By," 38

Colors
"Colours," 1

Cowboys
"Deep in the Heart of Texas," 5

Dreams
"Michael, Row the Boat Ashore," 9

England
"As Tears Go By," 38

Family
"Michael, Row the Boat Ashore," 9
"Shalom Chaverim (We Wish You Peace)," 30

GENRE/THEME INDEX

Feelings
"Colours," 1
"Rhythm Is Gonna Get You," 50

Folk
"Colours," 1
"Turn! Turn! Turn!", 26

Food and drink
"Take Me Out to the Ball Game," 13

Freedom
"Colours," 1
"Rock My Soul," 17

Good-bye
"Shalom Chaverim (We Wish You Peace)," 30

Helping
"Michael, Row the Boat Ashore," 9

Heroes and heroines
"Rock My Soul," 17

Home
"Deep in the Heart of Texas," 5

Hope
"He's Got the Whole World," 34

Imagination
"There's a Hole," 22

Israeli song
"Shalom Chaverim," 30

Jazz
"When the Saints Go Marching In," 42

Latin
"Rhythm Is Gonna Get You," 50

Life
"Turn! Turn! Turn!", 26

GENRE/THEME INDEX

Love
"Colours," 1
"Rock My Soul," 17

Nature
"Colours," 1
"Deep in the Heart of Texas," 5

Numbers
"Take Me Out to the Ball Game," 13

Peace
"Shalom Chaverim (We Wish You Peace)," 30

Relatives
"Michael, Row the Boat Ashore," 9
"Shalom Chaverim (We Wish You Peace)," 30

Rhythm
"Rhythm Is Gonna Get You," 50

Scotland
"Colours," 1

Seasons
"Turn! Turn! Turn!," 26

Sound
"Rhythm Is Gonna Get You," 50

Sports
"Take Me Out to the Ball Game," 13

Time
"As Tears Go By," 38
"Colours," 1
"Michael, Row the Boat Ashore," 9
"Turn! Turn! Turn!," 26

Work
"Michael, Row the Boat Ashore," 9

World
"He's Got the Whole World," 34

GRAMMATICAL INDEX

Use this index to look up a particular grammatical usage or verb tense that you want to practice. We have included examples from the Introductions, the Songs and from the Learning Ideas. When a song has many examples of a particular usage, we list one or two examples and then add "+ others."

Action Verbs
    to weep, to gather + others: "Turn! Turn! Turn!", 26

Adjectives
    big and bright, wide and high: "Deep in the Heart of Texas," 5
    the whole world, the little-bitty baby: "He's Got the Whole World," 34
    high, low, dark: "Rock My Soul," 17

  so + adjective
    so high, so low, so wide: "Rock My Soul," 17

  too + adjective
    it's not too late: "Turn! Turn! Turn!", 26

Adverbs
    I rarely use: "Colours," 1
    till we meet again: "Shalom Chaverim," 30
    I never get back: "Take Me Out to the Ball Game," 13

Antonyms
    big, high, rush, bright, wide, love: "Deep in the Heart of Texas" (Learning Ideas), 5
    wide, dark, safe, deep, over, behind, in: "Rock My Soul," (Learning Ideas), 17
    weep, reap, love, laugh, war, mourn: "Turn! Turn! Turn!", 26

Articles
  Definite
    the stars, the prairie sky: "Deep in the Heart of Texas," 5
    the boat: "Michael, Row the Boat Ashore," 9
  Indefinite
    a helping hand: "Michael, Row the Boat Ashore," 9

Can: see Modals

Colors
    green, yellow: "Colours," 1

GRAMMATICAL INDEX

Comparisons
  like
    the sage in bloom is like perfume: "Deep in the Heart of Texas," 5

Contractions
  bone's = bone is
    the toe bone's connected: "Dry Bones," 46
  can't = cannot
    so high you can't get over it: "Rock My Soul," 17
    my riches can't buy ev'rything: "As Tears Go By," 38
  don't = do not
    don't forget the poor: "Michael, Row the Boat Ashore," 9
    I don't care: "Take Me Out to the Ball Game," 13
  he's got = he has got
    he's got the whole world: "He's Got the Whole World," 34
  I'm I am
    I'm safe in the shadow: "Rock My Soul", 17
  it's = it is
    For it's one, two, three strikes: "Take Me Out to the Ball Game," 13
  that's = that is
    That's the time I love the best: "Colours", 1
  you're = you are
    you're out   "Take Me Out to the Ball Game," 13

Definite Articles: see **Articles, Definite**

Exclamation "Oh"
  Oh! rock my soul: "Rock My Soul," 17
  Oh, Lord I want to be + others: "When the Saints Go Marching In," 42

Expressions
  mm-hmm, uh-huh: "Colours," 1

Future Tense
  with "going to"
    Those bones are going to rise again: "Dry Bones," 46
    Rhythm is gonna get you: "Rhythm Is Gonna Get You," 50

Gerunds as Adjectives
  smiling faces, rain falling: "As Tears Go By," 38
  a helping hand: "Michael, Row the Boat Ashore," 9
  towering man, light shining: "Rock My Soul", 17

Gonna: see **Future Tense** with "going to" and **Reductions**

GRAMMATICAL INDEX

"Got" = has
  He's got the whole world: "He's Got the Whole World," 34

Imperative
  Affirmative
    hear the word of the Lord!:   "Dry Bones," 46
    Michael, row the boat + others: "Michael, Row the Boat Ashore," 9
    Throw the covers on your head: "Rhythm Is Gonna Get You," 50
    Rock my soul: "Rock My Soul", 17
    Take me out to the ball game + others: "Take Me Out to the Ball Game," 13
    Turn!:   "Turn! Turn! Turn!" 26
  Negative
    Don't forget the poor: "Michael, Row the Boat Ashore," 9

Indefinite Articles: see **Articles, Indefinite**

Like: see **Comparisons**

Modals
  Affirmative
    smiling faces I can see: "As Tears Go By," 38
    I can feel the light: "Rock My Soul," 17
  Negative
    My riches can't buy ev'rything: "As Tears Go By," 38
    You can't get over it: "Rock My Soul," 17

Non-Standard English
  never get back: "Take Me Out to the Ball Hame," 13
  it don't matter what you say + others: "Rhythm Is Gonna Get You," 50

Opposites: see **Antonyms**

Past Continuous
  Miami Latin Boys were playing: "Rhythm Is Gonna Get You" (introduction), 50

Past Tense
  songs sung by the British group
    + others: "As Tears Go By" (Introduction), 38
  he was eighteen years old when
    he made: "Colours," (Introduction), 1
  song sung by + others: "Michael, Row the Boat Ashore" (Introduction), 9
  Gloria Fajardo put a band together: "Rhythm Is Gonna Get You" (Introduction), 50
  was a camp meeting hymn + others: "When the Saints Go Marching In" (Introduction), 42

GRAMMATICAL INDEX

Phrasal (two-word) Verbs
   wipe away my pain: "Michael, Row the Boat Ashore," 9
   turn off all the lights: "Rhythm Is Gonna Get You," 50
   take me out, never get back: "Take Me Out to the Ball Game," 13
   build up, break down + others: "Turn! Turn! Turn!", 26
   when the moon goes down + others: "When the Saints Go Marching In," 42

Plural, Irregular
   I sit and watch the children play: "As Tears Go By," 38

Possessive
   the colour of my true love's hair: "Colours," 1

Prepositions
   in the heart of Texas + others: "Deep in the Heart of Texas," 5
   over it, around it, under it: "Rock My Soul," 17
   bump on the log in the hole + others: "There's a Hole," 22

Present Perfect Tense
   the time when I've been loved: "Colours," 1

Present Tense
Affirmative
   I sit and watch + others: "As Tears Go By," 38
   Yellow is the colour + others: "Colours," 1
   The stars at night are + others: "Deep in the Heart of Texas," 5
   We wish you peace: "Shalom Chaverim," 30
   There's a hole: "There's a Hole," 22
   sun refuses to shine + others: "When the Saints Go Marching In," 42

Contracted form
   that's the time: "Colours," 1
   I'm In the bosom: "Rock My Soul," 17
   it's one, two, three strikes: "Take Me Out to the Ball Game," 13

Negative
   I don't care: "Take Me Out to the Ball Game," 13

Reductions
   ev'rything, doin':   "As Tears Go By," 38
   mornin', sparklin', feelin', thinkin':   "Colours," 1
   gonna, 'bout: "Rhythm Is Gonna Get You," 50
   till we meet again: "Shalom Chaverim," 30

Rhymes
   deep, light, strong, wide: "Rock My Soul" (Learning Ideas), 17

GRAMMATICAL INDEX

's got
He's got the whole word: "He's Got the whole World, 34

"So" + adjective
so high, so low, so wide: "Rock My Soul," 17

Synonyms
mellow, rise, sparkling: "Colours" (Learning Ideas), 1

"There" as subject
There's a hole in the bottom of the sea: "There's a Hole," 22
There is a season: "Turn! Turn! Turn!", 26

"Too" + Adjective
It's not too late: "Turn! Turn! Turn!", 26

Two-word verbs: see Phrasal Verbs

"Used to" + Verb
things I used to do: "As Tears Go By," 38

Verb + to + Verb
I want to be in that number: "When the Saints Go Marching In," 42

SONG INDEX

This index lists each of the thirteen songs in Level One in alphabetical order.

	Page
As Tears Go By	38
Colours	1
Deep in the Heart of Texas	5
Dry Bones	46
He's Got the Whole World	34
Michael, Row the Boat Ashore	9
Rhythm Is Gonna Get You	50
Rock My Soul	17
Shalom Chaverim (We Wish You Peace)	30
Take Me Out to the Ball Game	13
There's a Hole	22
Turn! Turn! Turn!	26
When the Saints Go Marching In	42